The Let's Talk Library™

Let's Talk About When You Have to Have Your Tonsils Out

Melanie Apel Gordon

The Rosen Publishing Group's
PowerKids Press™
New York

*For all the children—past, present, and future—at Children's Memorial Hospital in Chicago.
MGordon, RRT*

Published in 2000 by The Rosen Publishing Group, Inc.
29 East 21st Street, New York, NY 10010

First Edition

Book Design: Erin McKenna

Photo Credits and Photo Illustrations: p. 4 by Kelly Hahn; p. 7 © Dallon Design/Custom Medical Stock; p. 8 by Donna Scholl; pp. 11, 19 by Les Mills; p. 12 by Seth Dinnerman; pp. 15, 20 by Carrie Ann Grippo; p. 16 © Michael Philip Manheim/International Stock.

Gordon, Melanie Apel.
    Let's talk about when you have to have your tonsils out / by Melanie Apel Gordon.
        p.   cm.
    Includes index.
    Summary: Discusses where and what the tonsils are, how they become infected, why some people have to have them removed, and what happens during a tonsillectomy.
    ISBN 0-8239-5418-8
    1. Tonsillitis—Juvenile literature. 2 Tonsils—Juvenile literature. [1. Tonsillitis. 2. Tonsils.] I. Title.
RF491.G67 1998
617.5'32—dc21   98-39854
                                                                                       CIP
                                                                                        AC

Manufactured in the United States of America

Contents

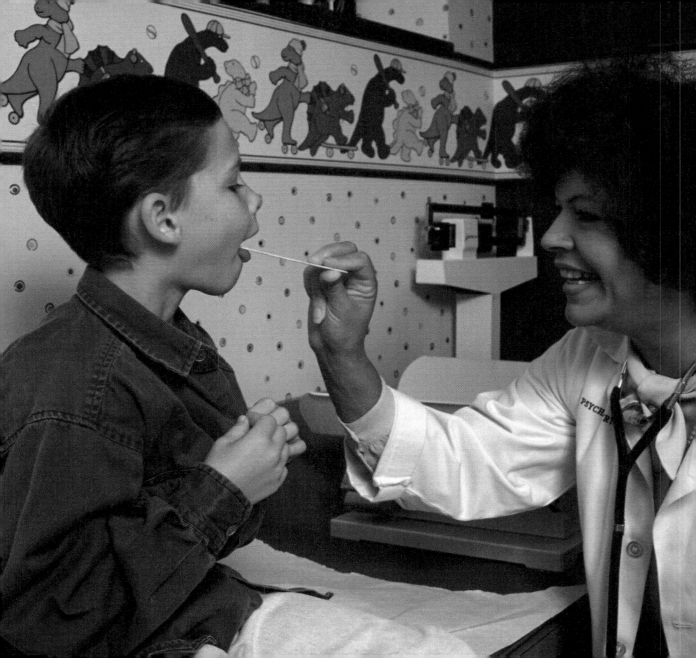

Jack's Sore Throat

Jack's throat has been sore a lot lately. Every time he gets a sore throat he has to stay home from school, take medicine, and drink lots of juice. Doctor Davies thinks Jack gets sore throats too often. Doctor Davies looks into Jack's throat to check his **tonsils**. They are red and swollen. Jack's tonsils are getting **infected,** which is causing his sore throats. Doctor Davies wants Jack to go to the hospital to have his tonsils taken out.

◀ Jack visits Doctor Davies a lot because of his throat.

Where Are Your Tonsils?

While looking in a mirror, open your mouth as wide as you can. At the back of your mouth, past your teeth and tongue, is your throat. The funny-looking thing hanging down in the middle of your throat is called a **uvula**. Look at the sides of your throat. On each side is a clump of **glandular tissue**. These clumps of **tissue** are your tonsils.

Your tonsils are the red tissue that sits on each side of your throat. ▶

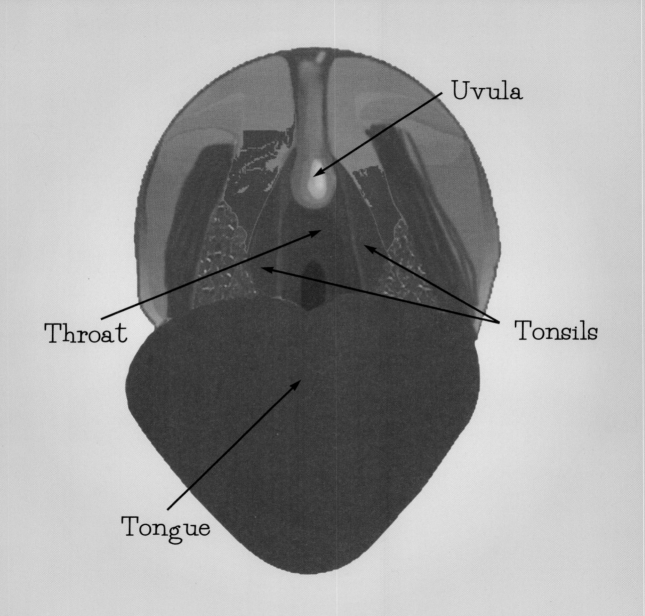

What Do Tonsils Do?

Once you are past the age of three, your tonsils don't do too much. Before that, however, tonsils have an important job. They stop **germs** that you breathe in before they can cause an **infection**. Tonsils help your body make special substances called **antibodies**. Antibodies are part of your body's **immune system**, which fights infection. The next time germs get into your body, your immune system will be able to fight them off with the help of antibodies.

◀ *Germs can get passed from person to person just by breathing or touching.*

Tonsillitis

Tonsils can get infected. When your tonsils are infected they turn bright red and get swollen. When this happens, you get a sore throat. This is called **tonsillitis**. Your tonsils may get so swollen that it's hard to eat. That's because there may not be enough room for the food to go down your throat. Your swollen tonsils might even make it hard for air to go down, so you may have a hard time breathing. Your doctor will give you medicine for tonsillitis.

If tonsillitis is making it hard to swallow, try eating soft foods and soups. They will go down more easily. ▶

Do I Need My Tonsils Out?

Medicine can usually make a tonsil infection go away. What if you keep getting lots of sore throats or throat infections? If you keep getting sick, your doctor will give you different medicines. If they don't work, and your throat keeps getting sore, your doctor may decide to take your tonsils out.

◀ *Getting sick over and over again is not good for your body.*

About the Hospital

If your doctor decides that you need to have your tonsils taken out, you will have an operation called a **tonsillectomy**. You'll have to go to the hospital for this. If you've never been in a hospital before, you may ask your doctor to take you on a hospital tour. You will be able to see the operating room where the **surgeon** will do your tonsillectomy. You will also see the **recovery** room where you will wake up after your tonsillectomy.

Going to the hospital might be scary. Don't worry, everyone there will take good care of you. ▶

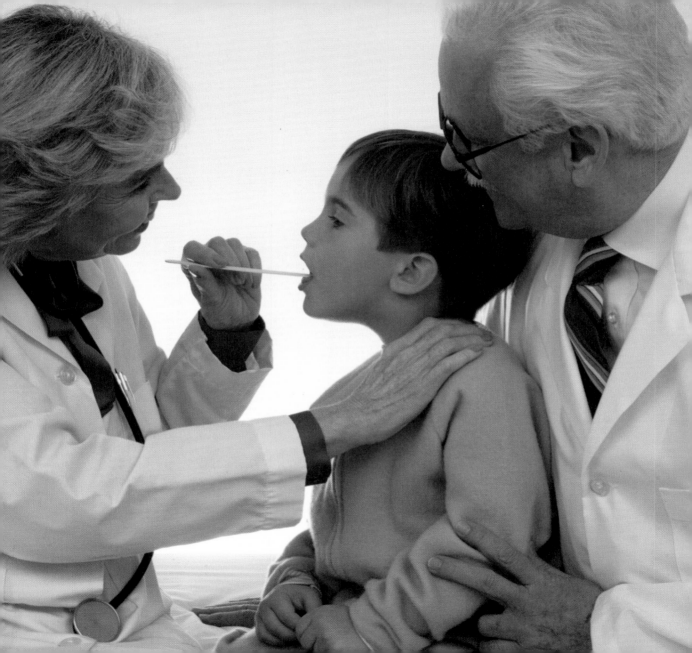

Surgery

Once you are in the hospital, your doctor will get you ready for the tonsillectomy. First you will have to take off your clothes and put on a hospital gown. Your doctor will give you special medicine, called **anesthesia**. Anesthesia will make you go to sleep for a little while. You will sleep through the entire operation. You won't feel the doctor take your tonsils out. When you wake up after surgery, your throat will be sore for a few more days.

◀ *Doctors will check your throat and your heartbeat before you go into surgery.*

Ice Cream!

Your throat will feel sore after your tonsillectomy. It may hurt when you try to talk. It may also hurt to swallow. There is one really good thing about the sore throat you will have after your tonsils are taken out. You will have to eat very soft foods, like ICE CREAM! You may also eat things like Jell-O gelatin, Popsicles, soup, and juice. All these things will slide easily down your throat while it heals.

It will hurt to swallow food right after your operation, even ice cream. Eating slowly will help. ▶

Adenoids

Sometimes you may get an ear infection along with a sore throat. This is because of your **adenoids**. Adenoids are located high in your throat behind your nose. Like your tonsils, adenoids are made of glandular tissue. They are connected to your ears. If your tonsils and adenoids get infected, you may also get an ear infection. If you've had a lot of ear infections your doctor may want to remove your adenoids when she removes your tonsils.

◄ *Your ears are connected to your throat. When one gets infected, often the other does too.*

Tonsil Facts

- About 400,000 kids have their tonsils taken out every year.
- Grown-ups don't usually need to have their tonsils taken out.
- Tonsils don't grow back.
- If you have to stay overnight at the hospital, your mom or dad can sleep at the hospital with you.

Ask your doctor all the questions you want about what is going to happen during and after your operation. Then you'll know what to expect. Remember that having your tonsils out will make your throat a healthier place!

Glossary

adenoids (A-duh-noydz) Glandular tissue behind your nose that is connected to your ears and throat.

anesthesia (a-nus-THEE-zhuh) Medicine to make you sleep through an operation.

antibody (AN-tih-bah-dee) Something made by your body to fight germs that cause infections.

germ (JERM) A tiny living thing that can cause sickness and infection.

glandular tissue (GLAN-juh-ler TIH-shoo) Groups of cells in the body that relate to glands, which are special organs.

immune system (ih-MYOON SIS-tem) The system in the body that fights infection and disease.

infected (in-FEK-ted) To have a disease that was caused by germs.

infection (in-FEK-shun) Any disease caused by germs.

recovery (rih-KUH-vuh-ree) Healing.

surgeon (SER-jun) A doctor who does operations.

tissue (TIH-shoo) Parts of the body that are formed by groups of cells.

tonsillectomy (tahn-suh-LEK-tuh-mee) The operation in which your tonsils are removed.

tonsillitis (TAHN-suh-LY-tus) When tonsils are red, sore, swollen, and infected.

tonsils (TAHN-sulz) Glandular tissue on the sides of your throat.

uvula (YOO-vyoo-lah) The piece of tissue that hangs in the back of your throat.

Index

A
adenoids, 21
anesthesia, 17
antibody, 9

B
breathing, 9
    trouble with, 10

E
eating, trouble
    with, 10

G
germ, 9
glandular tissue, 6,
    21

H
hospital, 5, 14,
    17, 22

I
ice cream, 18
immune system, 9
infection, 9
    ear, 21
    throat, 5, 10,
    13, 21

M
medicine, 5, 10,
    13, 17

O
operation, 14, 17,
    22

R
recovery room, 14

S
surgeon, 14
surgery, 17

T
throat, 6, 10, 18,
    21, 22
    sore, 5, 10,
    13, 17, 18,
    21
tissue, 6
tonsillectomy, 14,
    17, 18
tonsillitis, 10

U
uvula, 6